Girls' Guide
for Your

By Isabel & Emily Lluch

AND THEIR PANEL OF EXPERTS

WS Publishing Group
San Diego, California

❀ Table of Contents ....

Looking Your Best

Fun, flirty, and fabulous!

Being a girl can be really hard! Don't get us wrong, we would never trade it, but girls have a lot to think about, including our weight, what to wear, and our overall appearance. It's so weird to think how we were little girls not so long ago, and now we find ourselves out bra shopping!

★ Isabel's Perspective

Physical changes are confusing and nerve-wracking. On top of that, you have to worry about being stylish while outfitting your changing body. Every girl deals with this stuff differently. Learning how to dress for my body type has been very important. I mean, no one wants to see a too-tight outfit or some girl's underwear sticking out. So learning to trade popular trends for what looks good on your body is the first lesson in fashion.

The next lesson is to hold off the pressure to wear tons of makeup. I'm talking about heavy eye shadow, eyeliner, and dark lipstick. These make girls our age look like they're trying too hard. I was one of those girls who always put on too much makeup. Our beauty expert, Wendy McGill, helped me tone it down! She suggests wearing subtle, light colors for the "barely there" look. She said you want just enough to highlight your natural beauty.

★ Emily's Perspective

I agree that you wear too much makeup. LOL! I'm not as much a makeup girl—to me, being pretty is more about having great hair. Not all of us are born with it, but there are hair products that can totally fix poofy, flat, frizzy, crazy-curly, or limp hair. I also want to talk about the pressure girls encounter when it comes to fashion. Instead of trying to keep up with the fashionistas at your school, you should experiment with different styles until you find one that fits you.

Body Types

★ The Scoop

It's totally OK if you don't look exactly like other girls. I mean, we all come in different shapes and sizes. And though it may not always be easy to choose what to wear, understanding your individual body type will give you fashion direction.

Since you're not a kid anymore, it's time to start choosing clothes for your body type, instead of just throwing on whatever's on the floor. Pear-shaped girls are bigger on the bottom. Apple-shapes are broader on the top. Girls with the same size bust and hips are hourglass-shaped. And finally, some girls are a rectangle shape, meaning they are pretty much straight up and down.

According to our fashion expert, Wendy McGill, the most important component of any fashion sense is your attitude. She says, no matter what your size or shape, you should always carry yourself with confidence. If you look confident, you'll always look good.

★ May Ling's Question: Fit or Fat?

Lately I notice that my clothes are tight around the middle—especially my pants. It also seems like my shirt keeps riding up. I hate it, because it makes me feel like I'm getting fat! I still weigh the same, so I don't get it. How can I weigh the same but not fit into my normal clothes anymore?

Emily Says: I totally know how you feel! I play soccer, and when I grew out of my uniform, I freaked out thinking I was fat.

When I asked my coach about it she said that I was developing hips. She said my weight was shifting around. This is why even though I went up a whole pants size, I still weighed the same. Like my coach said, this means your body is just doing what it's supposed to do.

Did You Know?

Whenever you feel bad about your body, concentrate on what you're good at, playing sports, drawing, or singing. Remembering that you're really good at something that doesn't have to do with looks makes you feel awesome, instead of insecure.

Even though it stinks buying bigger clothes, it is the best option—don't stuff your new hips into old jeans. Once you get over the sticker shock of larger sizes, you'll look great.

Isabel Says: Emily's right; your body is filling out into its natural shape. Why don't you look at this as an excuse to get new clothes!

★ Katie's Question: Too Tall!

I have always been the tallest girl in my class. But now I tower over everyone, even the boys! Is it normal to be this tall? How can I make myself blend in more? I hate that I stand out so much.

Isabel Says: I feel you Katie—I was one of the tallest kids in my class for a long time. It's hard to be so tall, especially when you're bigger than most of the guys. But start thinking about being tall as a beautiful thing. I mean, it is the number one requirement in the modeling industry!

Emily Says: OK Katie, until your modeling career gets going, make small changes to accommodate your height. Don't slouch, because that lets everyone know you're uncomfortable—plus it's bad for your spine. You can wear flats, like tennis shoes or sandals to downplay your height, but I say, rock the heels anyway. If boys make jokes about your height, it's only because they wish they were taller!

> ### Fun Fact
>
> Curvy girls will look cute in dark pants that have a flare or boot cut leg. Jeans with tight ankles make girls with bigger butts look like inverted triangles, which is not a good look! Or, try a wrap-dress—they really flatter curvy bodies and are easy to accessorize. Also, wear shirts that reach your hips to give the illusion of a longer torso. Curves are feminine and pretty!

Isabel Says: Don't worry girlie—you won't always tower above everyone else. Your growth spurt just came before the others! The other kids caught up to me in about a year. Soon you'll be the one wearing heels to look taller!

Helpful Hint

We worry we are getting fat, however, most of us are just going through the normal filling-out process that happens during puberty. So, unless your current weight is 10 percent or more than what is recommended for your age and height, don't sweat it! Eat healthy and exercise and your body will even itself out.

☞ Expert's Point of View

Tips and Advice from Dr. Stuart Cohen

Though your body is going to change quite a bit over the next several years, your body type will always remain the same.

For example, if you are "big-boned," you will always weigh a little bit more than other girls your size. But this does not mean you are fat! Don't obsess over your weight, because the numbers on the scale can fluctuate from day to day depending on what time it is or how much water you've had to drink. Instead, focus on how your body looks proportionally. If your weight is distributed evenly, then you will look great, no matter what the scale says.

Accept that there is nothing you can do to change your body type, and then embrace it. Indeed, though your frame is determined by genetics, your attitude and level of physical fitness are most definitely up to you. These make all the difference in the way you look.

Fashion

It's hard to imagine having to think about one more thing besides our grades, friends, and relationships, right? Well, add "what to wear" to your list, because fashion choices can make or break a girl's entire look. So get schooled on how to dress, what not to wear, and what works for your body type.

Shopping for clothes doesn't have to break the bank. To save some bucks, shop at thrift stores. Vintage clothes are hip, chic, and unique. Look for cool stuff like cowboy boots, dresses from the '70s, and costume jewelry. A big plus is that thrifted clothes, like jeans, come perfectly broken in. Also, consider doing a monthly clothing swap with your girlfriends. This is fun and saves everyone money!

In fact, dressing for your particular shape is more important than any piece of clothing you put on your body. But being fashionable doesn't mean becoming a slave to the latest trends. This can get cheesy, not to mention expensive, when the styles change. Stock your wardrobe with mostly classic pieces and just a few trendy ones, and you'll always be in style. Examples include jeans, fitted t-shirts, a white button-down shirt, a fitted jacket, sandals, boots, and cute accessories. With these, your look will always be in.

Plus, when you don't know what to wear, you can just combine a few of these classic pieces to create a foolproof outfit!

★ Aleah's Question: Brand Names

I get that clothes matter, but the girls in my school act like the only thing that counts is "who" you're wearing. My parents won't buy clothes that cost a lot of money. I never cared before, but I'm starting to feel like a loser. How can I keep up with the fashionable girls in my school and still respect my parents' budget?

Isabel Says: There are some things parents do not understand, and the allure of designer labels on jeans and bags is definitely one of them. Luckily, you can find designer labels at stores like TJ Maxx, Ross, Marshall's, Off Fifth, and Nordstrom Rack. These stores sell name-brand clothing for much less. Also, cruise clearance racks at your favorite stores, and shop a season ahead or behind (i.e., get bathing suits at the end of the summer and save them for next year).

Girl to Girl

Every girl should own one great pair of boots. All boot styles look fabulous with jeans, skirts, and dresses. They can dress an outfit up or down, and will definitely make a girl look cool—especially if she's wearing cowboy boots with a skirt!

Emily Says: Hey Aleah, I totally get what you're saying—I loved this designer purse, but my parents said it was too expensive. I was so bummed! Try showing your parents how well you take care of your things and they may be more inclined to splurge on one item for your birthday, for instance.

★ Ashanti's Question: Size 14

I wear a size 14 and have trouble finding cool clothes that look good on me. I hate going shopping, because my mom always takes me to old-lady stores. Is there anywhere I can shop that has stylish clothes in bigger sizes?

Isabel Says: Hi girlie! Don't freak out, there are a ton of cool stores and online sites for plus-sized girls. In fact, I just went shopping with my friend who is a size 16, and we had a great time! She found so many hot clothes and accessories. Since now the average American woman is a size 12 to 14, stores have stepped it up and meet the demand.

Emily Says: Ashanti, our fashion expert, Wendy McGill, says some great stores to find cool clothes in larger sizes are Torrid, Old Navy, Fashion Bug, and The Gap. And don't forget Target! There are also tons of trendy online stores, like www.alight.com and www.bandlu.com. When all else fails, buy simple clothes and complement them with stylish accessories and cute shoes.

Helpful Hint

Do you know why celebs' clothes always fit perfectly? They go to a tailor! The fact is, clothes are mass-produced from cookie-cutter patterns, so they don't fit everyone. But you can make your clothes look as if they were made for you by getting them tailored. If the dress you love fits perfectly in some spots but not others, take it to a seamstress and have it custom-fit for your body.

Isabel Says: Wendy also mentioned that all girls can tame problem areas by wearing body shapers. These will slim bellies, butts, and hips to create smooth lines beneath your clothes.

☞ Expert's Point of View

Tips and Advice from Wendy McGill

A lot of girls forget that fashion is supposed to be fun. Clothes and accessories are not just functional—they offer young women a way to express themselves. In fact, fashion is one way to be many different people all at the same time. You can be preppy one day and Goth the next. And in between these extremes, there are a million ways to create a visual presentation of who you are. Your style will always be evolving, and that is part of what's satisfying about building a wardrobe.

What is also interesting about fashion is that even when girls try a new look every few months, there are some core choices that appear over and over. These recurring fashion themes form a person's style. It's truly a delight to watch this process unfold!

Let your style take shape over time, and don't be in such a hurry to look like everyone else. It's the girls who dress uniquely that end up setting the trends.

Body Hygiene

Sugar and spice and everything nice...

Once puberty hits, there are so many things a girl has to deal with! And I'm talking about changes that are in addition to the regular stuff like periods and boobs. Around this time, many of us have to get braces, glasses, or retainers too, which can be a downer if you let it.

★ Emily's Perspective

It's not all bad—we also get to paint our nails and get our ears pierced! These are fun milestones that girls look forward to. But some stuff we have to deal with can make you cringe! One of the most embarrassing changes we face during puberty is developing weird body odors in super-private places. Smelling like a bag of onions after gym class is social suicide, so it must be avoided at all costs. This means taking showers, wearing deodorant, and changing our clothes often or dressing in layers. You may start wearing perfume, but don't think this is a substitute for good hygiene!

★ Isabel's Perspective

During puberty, there are some areas we need to start thinking more about, like the skin on our faces. Of course we all wash our faces in the morning, but how many of us also wash before going to bed? And I bet most of you don't wash your necks, shoulders, or backs. Well, get scrubbing girls because oils build up there too, and can cause nasty breakouts and "backne." Yikes!

We also need to remember to wash our feet—even between our toes—because unfortunately, foot odor comes with the whole puberty package. Other areas you might not think to wash are behind your ears and knees. Seriously! Sweat covers all of you and can really make you stink. Also, wearing the same shirt to softball practice without washing it will definitely alert the team that your hygiene habits need work.

Body Odors

Body odors are a fact of life that we all wish we could forget! But since we can't, we might as well get a handle on them by understanding where they come from.

Helpful Hint

If you wear polyester and rayon shirts, wear a little cotton tank top underneath your clothes. Cotton fibers absorb sweat and let your skin breathe, which means less stink. So go all-cotton for a natural way to limit your new smells. This is especially true for underwear!

And since stinky feet also come with the onset of puberty, invest in lots of cotton socks.

The first place you might notice a new smell is your armpits. Once puberty begins, sweat glands in your armpits become active. They pump out a mixture of sweat and chemicals that causes an unpleasant smell. Underarm odor may smell sickly sweet, or like garlic and onions. It depends on your body's particular chemistry and your diet.

Thanks to puberty and the changes it brings, your vagina may also have a new smell. Practicing good hygiene by bathing daily with a mild cleanser will prevent odors from becoming overpowering. However, some odor is normal and products like sprays, douches, and creams that promise to eliminate vaginal odors should always be avoided!

★ Kiki's Question: Deodorant?

I sweat a lot, and I've been getting pit stains. It's really embarrassing, but what's worse is that I also have serious B.O.! One of my friends said I should wear deodorant, but there are so many kinds. How do I know what kind to get?

Emily Says: I sweat so much during soccer! Luckily, you can deal with this problem pretty easily by understanding what deodorants do. Antiperspirants prevent you from sweating. If you sweat a lot, this is the right choice. Deodorants, on the other hand, keep you from getting all smelly. It sounds like you have issues with both sweating and odor, so you should look for a product that does both.

Helpful Hint

Your diet may stink! Caffeine, spicy foods, and meat increase perspiration. This doesn't mean you should avoid these items, but limiting your consumption may reduce sweating. Also, avoid onions and garlic since they increase the B.O. factor.

☞ Expert's Point of View

Tips and Advice from Dr. Stuart Cohen

Body odor is a natural part of puberty and not a cause for concern. However, if frequent bathing and over-the-counter deodorants don't work, see your doctor. In some rare cases, severe body odor is a sign of a bacterial infection.

Skin Care

★ The Scoop

Your skin is your body's largest organ. It is also your defense system against injury, infection, and temperature change. It protects your internal organs from sun damage and helps rid you of toxins through perspiration. Skin is also your connection to touch. And, the way it forms over your bones gives you your unique appearance. With such important jobs, your skin needs to be cared for on a daily basis!

Getting into a skin care groove is easy and doesn't have to take more than 10 minutes a day. Start by using a gentle cleanser to keep your skin free of bacteria and pollutants. Moisturize dry areas—particularly your face, hands, elbows, knees, and feet—and get in the habit of wearing sunscreen every day. You will be so glad you used moisturizer and sunscreen when you are older, as dry, sun-exposed skin is the number one cause of wrinkles. The sooner you start caring for your skin, the better you'll hold up as the years go by.

★ Emani's Question: Bumps

I started getting these ugly little bumps on my fingers a few months ago. They're gross and it seems like whenever I scratch one away a bunch more appear in that spot! What the heck are these and what can I do to get rid of them?

Isabel Says: Ugh, it sounds like you've got warts! Dermatologist Dr. Fitzpatrick says you can get warts from touching someone else who has them. In other words, warts are contagious. Luckily, they can be treated. Start by putting an over-the-counter cream with salicylic acid on them. If they don't go away, your doc may freeze them using liquid nitrogen (cool!) or remove them by cutting them or burning them off.

Did You Know

Cold sores are caused by the HSV-1 virus, which is very contagious. So don't share lip balms or drink from others' cups. Though they can be painful and look gross, most cold sores will go away on their own within about 10 days.

☞ Expert's Point of View

Tips and Advice from Dr. Richard Fitzpatrick

Smart food choices help skin look great. Eating cantaloupe, carrots, sweet potatoes, spinach, blueberries, nuts, and beans protects skin from UV rays and helps it to heal faster. Also, foods like asparagus help skin retain elasticity.

Teeth

Appear cool and confident each time you flash your pearly whites by practicing excellent oral hygiene.

The most important tool in your repertoire is your toothbrush. Brushing your teeth for 3 minutes twice a day is the most effective way to remove bacteria and plaque from your tooth enamel. Enamel protects the inner, soft part of your teeth, called the pulp. Using soft bristles to brush your teeth prevents erosion of the enamel, which is a good thing, because the pulp it protects contains nerves that send pain signals to your brain. If you've ever had a cavity, you know what I mean! So brush to avoid pain and visit your dentist regularly.

Another way to keep your teeth healthy and pain-free is to floss once a day. Flossing daily dislodges muck and reduces your risk of cavities. Plus, it keeps your breath fresh, which is important should you find yourself kissing someone! LOL!

Helpful Hint

To keep your teeth healthy and strong, limit the amount of sugar in your diet. When left to sit on your teeth, sugar turns acidic and wears away enamel.

Sugar also makes your teeth susceptible to plaque and cavities. It is especially important to cut out sugary beverages, such as soda, since just 1 can of non-diet soda contains up to 10 teaspoons of sugar!

★ Abbey's Question: Braces

My dentist told me to see an orthodontist to find out if I need braces. I'm not sure I want braces though. They look like they hurt and some kids have to wear them for forever! How do braces work and how long would I have to wear them?

Emily Says: I have braces, and they're not a big deal. Braces work by putting pressure on your teeth to make them straight. They're brackets that are bonded to each tooth and connected by a wire. About once a month, your orthodontist will tighten the wire, which forces your teeth to move a little straighter. Your mouth will be sore for a few days, but you get used to it. What do you think, Isabel?

Girl to Girl

If you're on the go and don't have time to brush, swish some water around inside your mouth after drinking soda or juice, then spit it out. This will at least rinse sugar and stain-causing liquid off your teeth until you can get home and brush.

Isabel Says: I know braces can feel like they take forever, but they have to work slowly so you're not dying from the pain of wrenching your teeth. You'll only have them for about 2 years, which is a small price to pay for a gorgeous smile.

They shouldn't hurt too much day to day, but if your braces cut your mouth, you should ask for orthodontic wax. This coats the brackets and lets them slide along soft tissue inside your mouth.

★ Kiki's Question: Drilling

I just found out I have to have 2 cavities filled, and I'm freaking out! I could hear a drill in the other room and it sounded horrible! Do I have to get my cavities filled? Can't I just brush more often instead?

Isabel Says: Kiki, I'll give you the bad news first—you do have to get those cavities filled. My dentist, Dr. Hirsh, says that cavities form holes in your teeth. If you don't get cavities fixed, they cause nasty things like severe root pain, infections, and even bone loss.

So, since we both know you don't want any of that to happen, you're going to have to suck it up and face the drill. Which brings me to the good news: you won't feel it! Your dentist will numb your gums with a gel and then inject an anesthetic near your tooth so you won't feel a thing.

Helpful Hints

You can do something about gross bad breath! When brushing and flossing your teeth, don't forget to brush your tongue. Think of all the muck that gets absorbed in the thousands of taste buds that coat your tongue! Brushing your tongue and using mouthwash 1 or 2 times a day will give you fresh breath. This will give you confidence during close encounters of any kind.

Emily Says: After you get your cavities filled, be sure to brush and floss regularly to avoid getting another one.

Even though you're brushing and flossing, Dr. Hirsh says to have your teeth professionally cleaned twice a year (you may step this up to 4 times a year if you have braces). Dentists can clean down where your toothbrush can't!

Helpful Hints

After your braces are removed, you will be fitted for a retainer. Wearing a retainer helps your mouth "retain" all of the work braces did to your teeth and gums. Retainers are nearly invisible to other people. They are first worn for most of the day, and then only at night.

Expert's Point of View

Tips and Advice from Dr. Gary Hirsh

The best advice I can offer (besides brushing regularly, of course) is to get at least 1,300 milligrams of calcium every day until you turn 18.

Research shows that calcium plays a big role in having strong, healthy teeth and gums. Consider that your bone mass—which includes teeth, since teeth are bone—is at its peak around age 20. As you get older, your bones and teeth become weaker and more prone to breakage. So having a strong foundation is key for long-term dental and skeletal health.

It is best to get calcium from foods such as low-fat dairy products, dark green vegetables, nuts, and fortified cereals and juices. And watch your sugar intake—and not just with candy and soda, but with fruits and juices too. These have tons of sugar and can hurt your teeth. You should not avoid eating fruit, but definitely brush soon after chomping on that apple.

Feet

Put your best foot forward by keeping your feet clean, well-groomed, and beautiful!

Helpful Hints

Prevent athlete's foot by always wearing flip-flops in public showers, because this gross condition is caused by a contagious fungus. Yuck! Also, always dry them completely and allow your feet to be exposed to the air.

When you wear shoes, wear cotton or wool socks because they allow your feet to breathe and absorb moisture.

Think about how much your feet do for you every day. For example, they carry your entire weight (plus backpacks and books) from here to there. Yet, you probably don't give them a second thought except to wash them in the shower. Well, it's time to change the way you view your feet.

One of the best ways you can care for your feet is to wear the right shoes. Shoes that fit properly should not be too snug or loose. They should be supportive, have a low heel, and let your feet breathe. Pair your shoes to your activity. This means wearing cleats when you play soccer, and running shoes when you jog or exercise.

Truly, our feet do a ton for us. Sit back, relax, and put your feet up while you read on.

★ Emani's Question: Stinky Feet

Every time I have to take my shoes off in front of other people I get so embarrassed, because my feet stink so badly! I thought it was my shoes, but I got a new pair and my feet still smell. I shower every day, so why do my feet reek like rotten onions?!

Isabel Says: Your problem literally stinks! I am guessing this smell appeared out of the blue. You may have to wash your feet more than once a day and use baby powder to keep them dry. Also, try spraying disinfectant in your shoes. And definitely don't wear shoes without socks! Give your feet plenty of air time; keeping them dry and clean should cut the stench.

Helpful Hints

Soften your feet by using a weekly foot scrub. Make your own by mixing almond oil with sugar or sea salt. Rub it into your heels and the outer edges of your feet. Let it sit for 2 minutes before rinsing your feet with warm water.

👉 Expert's Point of View

Tips and Advice from Dr. Stuart Cohen

Part of taking care of your feet means watching your step, especially when walking barefoot. Stepping on glass or a nail hurts and may require a painful tetanus shot or even stitches. Even a stubbed toe can leave an unsightly bruise.

Puberty

We're in this together!

When our mom told us that going through puberty meant we would break out, bleed once a month, get cramps, have mood swings, develop breasts, have to wear a bra, grow hair in crazy places, gain weight, and cry for no reason, we nearly passed out!

★ Isabel's Perspective

T rust me, I begged her to not make me go through it. I tried to find a way around the whole thing. I thought maybe I could go from being a kid straight into adulthood without having to go through puberty. But finally I learned that it happens to all girls.

Then, one of my friends (who is 17) told me, "Going through puberty makes you smarter because you have to learn so much so fast." Once my body started changing, I learned about biology and even a few things about relationships, emotions, and love.

★ Emily's Perspective

W atching Isabel freak out, made me realize that I wasn't the only girl who was feeling scared about going through puberty. That was a huge step toward accepting the changes beginning to happen to my body. Of course, it's easy to forget you're not alone because what's happening to our bodies is so private. We grow hair on our vaginas and under our arms and develop boobs! Who wants to talk about THAT stuff?! I felt embarrassed, like a total freak. But after awhile, I got more comfortable talking to my mom, my sister, my older friends, and my doctors about this stuff—their perspectives totally helped me feel less alone.

Definitely do yourself a favor and find 1 or 2 older girls or women to talk to—your mom or your friends —because no one should have to go through puberty alone!

Acne

★ The Scoop

During puberty, your body releases hormones that tell the oil glands in your face, neck, chest, and back to wake up! These oil glands make your skin greasy, which traps bacteria and pollution. All this junk clogs your pores, which causes acne— both whiteheads and blackheads.

Girl to Girl

If acne makes you feel embarrassed, ashamed, or upset, it's time to ask your parents to see a dermatologist. There is no reason to allow breakouts to control your happiness or social life. Once you start the right treatment, you should see positive results within a few weeks.

Treatments include office visits, topical creams, and possibly oral medication. Treatment takes time, so be patient and give medications time to do their jobs.

You're probably thinking, "It's not fair! My skin was flawless a minute ago!" But don't worry, you aren't alone. According to the American Academy of Dermatology, almost 100 percent of teens break out. And 40 percent have severe enough breakouts to need medical help. For most girls, though, breakouts taper off around 5 to 10 years after the onset of puberty. So you can expect clear skin again in your 20s.

Remember, having a few breakouts doesn't mean you have to become a full-fledged crater face. You can contain zits before they become a total disaster!

★ **Ashanti's Question: Pizza Face**

I have pretty bad breakouts about once a month. My skin starts to feel extra greasy and my whole face turns into one giant zit factory! Why does this keep happening? Is it because of all the pizza I eat?

Fun Facts

Some pimple creams are flesh-colored, which is great, because they zap zits and cover them up without causing flare-ups.

Isabel Says: Don't worry girl, our dermatologist Dr. Fitzpatrick says breakouts don't have anything to do with eating chocolate or greasy food like pizza. Just don't touch your face if you have greasy, dirty hands!

It sounds like you're getting breakouts right before your period. Dr. Fitzpatrick says this is because of "hormone surges." Ugh! Pimples are just the icing on the cake of a really hard week!

Emily Says: I just started getting my period, Ashanti, and I totally know how you feel. Before my period I make sure to keep my hair out of my face. Oh, and you should wash your face both in the morning and before bed, since oils really tend to build up throughout the day and while you're asleep.

Isabel Says: One last thing Ashanti—drink plenty of water. That can help reduce breakouts too.

★ Abbey's Question: Body Breakouts

This is so gross to admit, but after every volleyball game, I get pimples on my chest and back, especially right where my sports bra straps are. I'm too embarrassed to wear tank tops now! What can I do to stop breaking out on my body?

Emily Says: Ugh! I hate when I get "backne" after a soccer game. It's so frustrating. Dr. Fitzpatrick suggested that I wear loose-fitting shirts when I can, since tight clothing can trap dirt in your skin. I like "dry-fit" tops, which soak up sweat and keep it off your skin.

Isabel Says: Abbey, the skin on your back is tougher than the skin on your face or chest, so it might take a more hard-core cleanser. Luckily, there are some good cleansers designed specifically for "backne," so grab one the next time you go grocery shopping.

Emily Says: Good point Isabel. Abbey, your chest is more sensitive, so don't over-scrub it. Just use your regular facial cleanser

Girl to Girl

Breakouts are huge bummers, but don't squeeze, pop, or pick at zits. This makes skin really irritated and usually makes the pimple redder, crusty, and more noticeable. Plus, picking and popping spreads bacteria and encourages more breakouts! Besides, if you pop a zit and it starts to bleed, it gets really nasty.

and be sure to shower after your volleyball games. Keeping fresh and clean will prevent body breakouts from popping up in the first place.

☞ Expert's Point of View

Tips and Advice from Dr. Richard Fitzpatrick

What's the truth about acne? Well, first, there is virtually no evidence to support the claim that sweets or greasy foods cause acne. Second, acne is not necessarily caused by poor hygiene, though additional oil from greasy hair and fingers can cause breakouts to become irritated. Third, stress can actually aggravate acne. Stress is an inflammatory response in the body and causes the adrenal glands to go into overdrive, leading to breakouts.

However, know that you are not powerless over pimples. There are many over-the-counter creams that are very effective. And dermatological treatment is an excellent way to manage mild to severe bouts of acne.

Finally, if you find yourself in the midst of an acne emergency, such as a huge pimple right before a school dance, see your dermatologist. He or she can use a cortisone injection to reduce the size and redness of a pimple in as little as 24 hours.

Periods

★ **The Scoop**

First zits and body odor, now periods! The arrival of your period is the main event for girls during puberty, and signifies that you're really becoming a woman. Although this can be a confusing and scary time for us, it doesn't have to be. By learning what causes your body to menstruate once a month, you are taking an important step in learning how to care for your new body.

Periods are a nuisance, but they are a natural part of growing up. You might view puberty as laying the groundwork for later on—when you are older and ready for grown-up stuff like pregnancy.

Most girls get their first period between the ages of 9 and 16. Once you get your first period—called menarche—you have entered your childbearing years. This means that starting now, your ovaries will release an egg each month in a process called ovulation. The egg travels through your fallopian tubes toward your uterus. Meanwhile, your uterus develops a thick lining called an endometrium. This lining houses and nourishes the egg, and would allow it to grow into a baby if sperm were present to fertilize it. When pregnancy occurs, women are without their periods for 9 months!

However, for the majority of your life, the egg will not be fertilized, so your uterus sheds the endometrium, blood, and egg.

These fluids exit your body through your vagina in a reddish-brown blood-and-fluid mixture that is called your period.

On average, your period will last about 5 days, although some may be as short as 2 days or as long as 7 days. Ovulation usually occurs 2 weeks before you get your period. These weeks are all part of what is called your menstrual cycle. Your monthly cycle may be set up so that you get your period every 28 days, which is the average for most girls. However, girls' periods might show up as early as every 20 days or as late as every 35 days. And many girls have irregular periods, sometimes skipping a month here and there—especially in the beginning. It just depends on your particular body's biological clock. However, if your period stays irregular for more than a few cycles, let your parents or doctor know.

Go With The Flow

Don't get caught off-guard by your first period! Know what to expect and what supplies you need. Now that you know why you get your period, the best way to deal with menstruation is to be prepared. After all, getting your period at school while wearing a white skirt would be awful! So keep an eye on your cycle by keeping a period calendar. Tracking when you last got your period will help you predict when it will come again. When you think your period might be on its way, put some tampons or pads in your backpack, purse, or locker. It's best to always be ready, since your period may not be regular in the beginning. Plus, carrying extras lets you to come to the rescue should a friend find herself in need!

★ Katie's Question: First Period Coming?

I'm so scared that I am going to get my period any day now! And when I do I will have no idea what to do! I live with my dad, and there's no way I can ask him about this stuff. What should I do and who should I ask? I don't even know how to use a pad or what to do with one once I'm done with it.

Isabel Says: Katie, if you think you are going to get your period soon then you probably are. I mean, doctors always tell us that we know our bodies best, right?

There are lots of ways to learn what to do—reading this book is a great first step! A good person to talk to is your school nurse. She will have supplies in her office in case you're surprised by your period when you're at school. And if you're too scared to talk to her, ask a friend to ask her mom to help.

Girl to Girl

You might feel pretty bloated right before and during your period. Avoid eating salty foods because sodium will make you retain water. But remember, drinking water dilutes sodium, so stay hydrated! Also, exercise will help you feel better, so get moving.

Emily Says: Hey Katie! I started with pads until I got comfortable using tampons. Pads have a sticky bottom and little side flaps, which keep them in place in your underwear. When you're done with one, just fold it up, wrap some toilet paper around it, and toss it in the trash.

★ May Ling's Question: Tampons

I am way too embarrassed to ask my mom how to use tampons, but I want to try them. I like to swim a lot in the summer, and I obviously can't wear pads in the water. Help! How do I put a tampon in?

Isabel Says: Don't panic, May Ling! Tampons are easy to use once you get the hang of them.

First, either sit on the toilet or put one foot up on the bathtub. Hold the tampon in the same fingers you write with and make sure the string sticks out of the applicator. This part is embarrassing, but do it anyway: Open up your vaginal lips with

❀ Inserting a Tampon • • • • • • • • • • • • • • • • • •

Step 1:

Hold the plastic applicator between your thumb and middle finger (you will use your first finger to push the tampon in). Find a comfortable position—some girls like to stand with one foot up, such as on the edge of the bathtub, or sit down with knees spread.

Step 2: With the hand not holding the applicator, pull open the folds of skin around the vaginal opening. Position the rounded tip of the tampon (not the end with the string) against your vaginal opening.

your other hand and insert the tampon. Push it up and stop once your hand touches your vagina. Then, push the applicator all the way up. Congrats girl—it's in!

Remove the applicator, toss it in the trash, wash your hands, and you're in business.

Emily Says: Isabel makes it sound easy, but she was actually too squeamish to show me (thanks sis!). I was so freaked out to use tampons, but I figured it out with a little practice. Just relax or you'll tense up, which will make things even more difficult.

Start with a small-sized tampon. Practice a few times, and if you mess up, it's easy to start over.

Step 3: The vagina slants at an angle, so you should slide the applicator in gently, tilting it at an upwards and backwards angle. It will help to stay relaxed when you ease the applicator in. Stop pushing when the fingers holding the applicator meet your body.

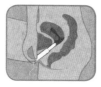

Step 4: Now that the applicator is inserted, use your first finger to push the bottom of the small tube completely up inside the big tube. This slides the tampon into your vagina, leaving the string outside your body. Then, simply pull out the plastic applicator, wrap it up, and throw it in the trash.

★ Ashanti's Question: Cramps!

I seriously have the worst cramps in the universe when I get my period. I can barely get out of bed, they're so painful! I've tried a bunch of over-the-counter pain relievers and nothing seems to do the trick. I end up staying home from school for like 2 days when I get my period. Is there anything that will get rid of really bad cramps so I don't have to miss so much school?

Emily Says: Cramps are such an unfair part of the whole period thing, aren't they? I'm really sorry you get such bad ones Ashanti, but there are ways to make it so you can still go to school. It's really important that girls know we don't have to be in pain.

Girl to Girl

Wear panty liners a few days before and after your period in case it shows up early or to catch spotting afterward. And don't stress—light spotting between periods is totally normal!

For starters, talk to your doctor about prescription painkillers or muscle relaxers. Dr. Cohen also recommends using a heating pad for a half-hour when cramps are at their worst. Plus, even though you don't feel like it, exercise. It totally cuts down on the pain.

Isabel Says: Ashanti, Dr. Cohen also says that if you ever have sharp pains in your abdomen, soak more than 2 pads in an hour, or bleed for 10 days or more, see a doctor right away.

★ Aleah's Question: Tampons & Virginity

A girl in my gym class said that if I use tampons I won't be a virgin anymore because they can break your hymen. I want to start using tampons on a regular basis, but not if that's true! Help!

Isabel Says: Don't worry, Aleah—you can definitely use tampons and still be a virgin. In reality, virginity has to do with sexual intercourse and nothing to do with inserting a tampon.

Besides, you shouldn't stress so much about tearing your hymen. According to Dr. Cohen, your hymen is a just very thin layer of tissue that partially covers the opening to the vagina. He says it's so fragile that a lot of girls will naturally stretch or tear their hymens during sports or other physical activities.

Emily Says: So true, sis. Lots of girls start using tampons when they're pretty young because they play a sport or swim. I think tampons are great—once you get the hang of them, you can't feel them at all. They're actually comfortable! Of course, Aleah, using tam-

Girl to Girl

Toxic shock syndrome (TSS) is a rare but serious condition that can develop from using tampons. When used improperly, tampons can introduce bacteria to your body that can lead to TSS. To avoid TSS, change your tampon every 4 to 8 hours. Use the smallest size tampon to handle your flow. Make sure your hands are clean when you insert a tampon, and never use tampons when you do not have your period.

pons is totally up to you, but it sounds like you're ready for them. So don't listen to that myth about tampons—now you know the truth!

Expert's Point of View

Tips and Advice from Dr. Stuart Cohen

The week before your period you may feel like you are losing control over your emotions. Don't worry ladies, you are not crazy! You're just like millions of girls—3 out of 4 women, in fact—who suffer from premenstrual syndrome (PMS). Though no one knows exactly what causes PMS, doctors attribute it to changing hormone levels.

Usual symptoms of PMS include mood swings, food cravings, depression and bouts of crying, aches and pains, and acne. However, if your symptoms are severe enough to prevent you from engaging in normal activities, talk to your doctor. In some cases, PMS symptoms highlight underlying depression. This can make symptoms unmanageable and a doctor's treatment is required.

However, for the majority of girls, PMS is fleeting and manageable with rest, good nutrition, exercise, over-the-counter pain relievers—and patience!

Breasts

★ The Scoop

The first stage of breast development occurs before puberty begins when your chest is flat and there is little color in the nipple area.

The second stage starts at puberty when little breast buds form beneath both nipples. Also, the circles around your nipples—called areolas—will darken and spread.

The third stage is a continuation of the second—breasts get a bit larger, nipples stick out more, and areolas become darker.

The fourth stage of breast development is when a tiny mound rises out of the breast, though many girls skip this and go straight to the final stage.

In the fifth and final stage of development, breasts take on a round, full shape with darkened areolas and raised nipples. This stage is usually completed when a girl is about 17 years old.

Fun Fact

Many girls' breasts develop so that one is smaller than the other. This is 100 percent normal, so don't feel weird if it happens to you! In fact, many times one side develops its breast bud up to 6 months before the other.

Your breasts will probably catch up to each other, but if there is a big size difference that bothers you, wear an insert in your bra to even out their appearance.

★ Katie's Question: Flat-chested

My boobs are so small, it's depressing. I don't get it, because my mom has pretty big boobs, and so does my sister. When are my boobs going to grow, and how can I tell how big they will be?

Fun Fact

Before you beg mom and dad for breast implants, consider this: A study found that 40 percent of women who have this surgery end up with a serious complication within 3 years. Also, many women require more surgeries within 5 to 10 years.

Emily Says: Aw Katie, I know how you feel! Isabel has big boobs, so I figured I would too—but it hasn't happened so far! The thing is, it's impossible to predict, because your breast size is not based on your mom's or sister's sizes. But once you get your period, who knows how big they might get! My advice is to find a bra with a little bit of padding until you develop more. Also, empire-waist shirts can make your boobs look bigger.

Isabel Says: Big boobs definitely aren't always better. I was a C cup in middle school and I was miserable. Boys picked on me and some girls were nasty, too. I eventually learned to like being curvy, but lot of girls probably wish their boobs were smaller like yours.

Emily Says

I think small boobs are cute. Models always have small chests!

★ Abbey's Question: Lumpy Breasts

My boobs are still pretty small, but they feel really lumpy! I know lumps can sometimes mean breast cancer, so I'm kinda freaked out. Should I tell my mom or my doctor?

Emily Says: Don't worry Abbey! Dr. Cohen says that most girls and women have some natural lumpiness in their breasts. So this is totally normal!

The most important thing, he says, is to do a Breast Self Exam, or BSE, often, so you are familiar with how your breasts feel normally. That way you will know if anything weird starts happening in the future.

Isabel Says: I had this exact same question, Abbey. My breasts get really lumpy, especially during my period. But now that I know it happens to most girls, I don't worry so much.

Girl to Girl

Have you noticed red lines on the sides of your breasts or hips? If so, you have stretch marks. Though they're not the prettiest body accent, they are common and harmless. Stretch marks are a side effect of your skin stretching as your body develops. While you can't get rid of them, you can make them less noticeable by moisturizing with cocoa butter.

You're probably still too young to have to do frequent BSEs, but in a few years, you'll want to do one every month or so. Lumps you can move around, or a pebbly, grainy texture are normal, but if you notice a bump that seems harder or larger than the others, tell your doctor. It's always smart to get an expert's opinion.

Growing tissue causes skin to stretch, which can make your chest dry. To reduce itching and redness, put lotion on your breasts after you shower, while you are still damp, to lock in moisture. For particularly itchy skin, take lukewarm baths with a dash of olive oil in the water.

☞ **Expert's Point of View**

Tips and Advice from Dr. Stuart Cohen

Start developing habits that promote healthy breasts now. Eating a diet rich in fruits and vegetables and low in fat provides your breasts with ammunition to ward off cancer.

In addition, get in the habit of examining your breasts regularly for abnormal lumps and bumps. Give yourself a breast exam in the shower. Raise your arm above your head and feel around your breast for anything suspicious.

You are also never too young to avoid habits that are damaging to breasts. One habit to avoid is smoking. Smoking within 5 years of getting your first period nearly doubles your risk of getting breast cancer as an adult! This is because your breast tissue is still developing and is easily damaged by toxins in cigarettes. Also, smoking depresses estrogen levels, which is bad for your developing body. So give your breasts a fighting chance and stay away from cigarettes!

Bras

Going from a t-shirt-only existence to having to wear a bra can be a big change. But choosing a bra doesn't have to be scary or embarrassing. You just need to learn the right style and fit for your particular size. Bras come in 6 basic styles: training bras, soft-cup, underwire, push-up, padded, and sports bras.

Helpful Hint

When you decide to buy a bra, your goal is to find one that fits, is comfortable, and gives the right amount of support. Understanding this is your first step! Then, ask your mom, aunt, or sister to take you bra shopping.

Next, dive in and try on bras. Grab a bunch of different sizes and styles and see which ones fit and look the best.

Most girls who are buying their first bra stick to training and sports bras. Training bras are perfect for preteens and girls whose breasts do not need much support. These are also designed for girls who do not yet fit in standard cup sizes. Another great option is the sports bra. This type of bra is very comfy, and gives a little more support than a training bra.

The most important feature of any bra is that you are comfortable wearing it!

★ Aleah's Question: Support

I need a bra with more support than my training bra. My sister and mom both wear underwire bras, but they look uncomfortable! How do I know what size and kind of bra to get next?

Isabel Says: Congrats Aleah—you've graduated out of your training bra! My mom told me to measure the amount of inches around your rib cage, just below your boobs, then add 5 to that measurement and round up to the next even number. This is the number portion of your size, such as 34. For cup size, you'll have to try different bras to find whether you're an A, B, C, D, etc. And don't worry, underwire bras are actually comfortable, supportive, and easy to get used to.

Helpful Hint

When buying a bra, choose one that fits on the outermost hook. As the bra stretches over time, you can simply hook it on one of the inner eyes. This ensures a good fit for a longer period of time! A bra you wear often will keep it's shape for about a year.

☞ Expert's Point of View

Tips and Advice from Dr. Stuart Cohen

There is no reason to wear a bra to bed. However, it will benefit you to wear a sports bra at night if your breasts are sore due to menstruation or development. The additional support minimizes pain caused by movement during sleep.

Hair Growth

Hair "down there" and in other new places is a perfectly normal part of puberty, it just takes a little getting used to. If you are like most girls, one day you looked in the mirror and noticed darker, curly hair growing on your vagina. This is one of the earliest signs that puberty has begun!

Hair grows in weird places during puberty due to hormones called androgens. Androgens also cause hair to grow under your arms and on your legs. This hair actually has a function; special hormones called pheromones cling to the hair. Humans have been using pheromones to attract mates since caveman times!

Helpful Hint

Sometimes, girls grow hair in areas more often seen on guys, like the chin, upper lip, and sides of the face. If this happens to you, do not shave with a razor! This will only make hairs that were light enough not to be noticed sprout up black and wiry when they grow back.

Instead, pluck with tweezers, wax them, or carefully bleach them with products designed for the face.

Body hair also protects sensitive areas from irritation and infection. However, it is OK to trim, shave, and pluck hair to look neat and groomed.

★ Katie's Question: Bikini Blues

I've got all this hair that pokes out of my bathing suit. It goes down to my knees. I didn't really care about it until someone made a joke. Now I want to get rid of it! What's the best way to go back to looking normal in a bathing suit?

Helpful Hint

Never shave your legs or armpits when they are dry! This will result in razor burn. Razor burn looks like a rash and may produce painful red bumps or really dry, itchy patches of skin. If you do get razor burn, try soothing products made with aloe vera gel or tea tree oil. Also, toss out your old, dull razors!

Isabel Says: Isn't it weird how everything is normal one day and the next, you feel like a gorilla? The area you're talking about is your bikini line and there are a couple of ways to deal with this. Although you can wax the area that runs along your bathing suit and down the insides of your thighs, this can be pretty painful. The best way to start is probably to shave.

Use a fresh razor and always shave in the direction that hair grows to reduce the chance of getting ingrown hairs, which are painful and look gross. If you're not ready to shave or wax, try wearing board shorts; they look cute and hide extra hair. My sister loves them!

Emily Says: Board shorts are a good option, Katie! Really, choose what is most comfortable for you—not what other people say!

★ **Emani's Question: Hair Trail**

This is so humiliating, but all of a sudden I've got hair in some really weird places. Like, I have this long trail of hair that goes down from my belly button! And hair under my arms. I feel like I look like a boy. Is this normal, and what can I do to get rid of it?

Emily Says: Emani, you are totally normal, don't even worry about it! Puberty does weird things to girls, and one of the weirdest is how much hair we get and where. Dr. Cohen says the hair under your arms is there to keep your skin from getting irritated. Shaving under your arms is really easy, and most American women do it.

Isabel Says: So true Emani—shaving your armpits is probably the easiest shave job you'll do! As for the hair under your belly button, it's sometimes called a "Happy Trail" (although I'm sure you're not happy about it). Turns out it's just an extension of your pubic hair. It's normal and common, so don't worry, you're not a boy! Try plucking dark hairs with tweezers.

Helpful Hint

Shaving your legs is easier if you do it after you've soaked in a warm bath or shower for awhile. This is because warm water makes skin softer and less prone to nicks, scrapes, and ingrown hairs.

For a smooth, clean shave, use shaving cream or gel rather than soap. When you are finished shaving, wait 20 minutes and put a light lotion on your legs to seal in moisture.

★ Aleah's Question: Growing Pains

Sometimes I wake up in the middle of the night and my legs are killing me! They throb and ache so bad that I can't go back to sleep. I'm too young for arthritis, right? That's what my grandma has, but that's what I think this feels like! What's wrong with my legs and how can I make it stop?

Isabel Says: Ouch! I went through this when I was 12 and I remember it killed. It feels like your bones are breaking apart!

Fun Facts

Both boys and girls release hormones called androgens that cause their voice boxes to grow larger. This has little effect on girls' voices, but don't be surprised if your guy friends' voices start cracking all the time!

Dr. Cohen says it's not the bones, but the muscles that ache. He said that 25 to 40 percent of all kids around this age get what are called "growing pains," and that for some reason it's worse at night.

Emily Says: Oh wonderful—something else to look forward to.

Aleah, Dr. Cohen also says to stretch before bed, massage your legs from the thighs down to your ankles, and use a heating pad.

Isabel Says: I know, isn't puberty great?

★ Marie's Question: Weight Gain

I have gained a lot of weight in the last year—15 pounds to be exact! And it seems like it's all in my butt and thighs. I feel like a real fatty, and now my jeans fit all weird. I am really athletic, and I'm not lazy or anything, so why is this happening?!

Emily Says: Marie, I promise this weight gain has absolutely nothing to do with being lazy. I play soccer pretty much every day and this is happening to me right now, too.

Nature says that women need to be wider through the hip area to be able to have babies. But since that's like a million years off, just don't let weight gain get out of hand. Keep up with exercise and don't chow on cheeseburgers every day at lunch. You will even out before you know it.

Isabel Says: Weight gain is one of the most shocking parts of puberty, in my opinion. I used to be rail-thin and now I have curves all over the place. It's weird watching

Did You Know

It's totally possible to grow as many as 4 inches in just 1 year! However, once you start having your period, you'll probably only grow another 3 or 4 inches total.

The average American woman is 5 feet 4 inches tall. But keep in mind height is a genetic trait, meaning that it is passed to you by your parents. If your parents are tall, you'll probably be too.

your body completely morph before your eyes!

The one thing that keeps me calm is knowing it's totally normal for girls to collect pounds in their stomach, hips, butt, and thighs. And I prefer my womanly body to my little girl body anyway!

👉 Expert's Point of View

Tips and Advice from Dr. Stuart Cohen

Some of the physical changes that accompany puberty are noticeably external, such as growing taller, wider, and gaining weight. But there are also many changes going on inside your body.

For example, the hormone "estrogen" causes your body to excrete a clear or white fluid from your vagina, called vaginal discharge. This helps your body flush out harmful bacteria. Another internal change is that your vaginal walls are becoming thicker. Your uterus and ovaries also get bigger.

You will also start ovulating regularly. Ovulation is the process in which your ovaries release the egg that gets flushed out with your period. Ovulation can feel like a slight pinching sensation for some girls, while others feel nothing. All these changes are preparing your body for the possibility of pregnancy when you are older.

Health Issues

Happy and healthy!

P uberty is insane—that's why it's important to take care of ourselves. Many girls don't realize that their bad habits make these tough times worse. Habits like eating junk food, sacrificing our skin to the sun, and staying up all night or sleeping all day are some ways we push our health aside.

★ Isabel's Perspective

We do this because we're invincible, right? Wrong! We're soooo not immune to getting sick or developing diseases.

Take scoliosis for example—though we can't control whether we get it, we can make sure we show up on testing day and follow our doctor's instructions on how to manage it. How many of us skip scoliosis screening because we're too embarrassed to line up in our bathing suits? Early detection is the only way to prevent scoliosis from getting worse.

★ Emily's Perspective

Right sis! It's true that a lot of unhealthy conditions can be prevented or improved by simply making better decisions. And when it comes to food choices, teens definitely need some major help. It seems like all we eat sometimes is fatty fast-food and candy and snacks. Turns out, there are so many things to learn about the food we eat—and it's actually pretty interesting stuff.

Consider the fact that every decision we make now will affect our bodies 40 years from now. That makes it a little easier to remember to throw on a hat to avoid a sunburn that could cause skin cancer! The same is true for food—eating fast-food every day will make you overweight, tired, and unhealthy. Not that you can't ever treat yourself to fries with ranch dressing once and awhile, but learning to live and eat in a healthy way is just the smart thing to do.

Eating Healthy

For many teens, it's easier to eat the same things every day, or just grab fast-food and pre-packaged junk food in a hurry. However, eating on the go most definitely contributes to this nation's growing obesity epidemic, because so little thought is given to portion size and nutrition.

Helpful Hint

Experts recommend that girls consume at least 1,300 milligrams of calcium per day. This is because about 25 percent of your bone mass will form after puberty.

Building strong bones can help prevent osteoporosis (a disease that causes bones to become weak) later in life. Foods rich in calcium include dairy products, tofu, almonds, and beans.

Think of food as fuel and your body as an expensive car. You wouldn't put cheap gas in a Mercedes, so don't fill your tank with junk food!

Plus, there are lots of important reasons for eating a low-fat, nutritious diet, such as reducing your risk of getting diabetes, heart disease, and painful joint conditions. Also, eating complex carbohydrates, lean proteins, fresh fruits and vegetables, and minimal sugar benefits your entire body—from your brain to your skin to your hair to your nails! Now is the time to develop healthy eating habits that will benefit you for years to come.

★ Haley's Question: Still Hungry!

I am trying to eat better, but when I have a salad for my meal it's not filling and I'm still hungry! The only time I actually feel full is when I eat stuff that's bad for me, like nachos and cheeseburgers. I want to eat healthier, but how can I when it doesn't ever fill me up?

Isabel Says: As a girl with an enormous appetite, I completely understand, Haley! Nutritionist Lisa K says to control hunger, it's actually better to eat small meals every 2 or 3 hours. This way, you end up eating 5 or 6 small meals a day, instead of 2 or 3 big ones.

I've been trying it and it works! Eating smaller meals of protein and fiber more often keeps me from feeling starved. That's good, because when you're starving, you tend to overeat. Plus, our physician, Dr. Cohen, says that eating more often keeps blood-sugar levels balanced and prevents afternoon crashes. So keep eating that salad, plus smaller portions of more substantial foods during the day.

Girl to Girl

Make your own trail mix with almonds, walnuts, raisins, dried cranberries, and other goodies. To maximize yumminess, use roasted, unsalted nuts. They're way better for you too!

Emily Says: Hey girl, I like eating hearty snacks like fruit and veggies, hummus and crackers, or nuts. They all have nutrients and fiber so you feel satisfied.

★ Emani's Question: Vegan

I'm vegan, which freaks my friends out because they are worried that I am malnourished! They're always trying to get me to eat meat and other animal products, which bugs me. But they are really worried, so I thought I should at least make sure I am not going to be super-short or stop getting my period or something.

Emily Says: You have to give your friends a break, Emani, because they obviously care about you. And some kids who go vegetarian or vegan don't understand that they have to eat more than just pasta and cookies. To be a healthy vegan, you really have to read labels carefully and make sure you get enough nutrients. Nutritionist Lisa K says as long as you do this, you'll be fine! Being a vegan who eats enough protein and calcium means you'll grow normally and, of course, still get your period.

Isabel Says: I actually decided to go vegetarian a year ago, Emani, so I know all about people freaking out. But I finally explained that

Helpful Hint

The number one reason people say they choose fast-food and pre-packaged snacks over fresh meals is because "it's easier." So remove the temptation, and increase the nutritional value of your food choices by planning ahead! It is easy to eat better if you do a little prep work. For example, cut fresh veggies and store them in ready-to-go baggies—then toss them in your backpack for a mid-morning snack.

★ Abbey's Question: 8 Cups?

I know I'm supposed to drink, like, 8 cups of water every day, but I cannot get that much water down! It just makes me gag after awhile. What's the smallest amount of water I can get away with drinking?

Emily Says: It depends on your activity level. I play sports, so I have to drink more water because I sweat so much. If you don't drink enough water to replace what you lost, your brain will get cloudy and your responses will be slow. I used to not like water either, but then I learned that a lot of foods contain water! So you can actually "eat" some of your 8 cups of water by snacking on oranges, watermelon, celery, and other fruits and veggies that are mostly water.

Helpful Hint

Though bottled water is marketed as "pure," it is often no better than tap water. A recent study found that one-third of bottled water has bacteria or chemicals in it! Instead, drink filtered tap water from a reusable polyurethane bottle.

☞ Expert's Point of View

Tips and Advice from Nutritionist Lisa K

Putting water back into your body is critical to its functioning, and also increases your overall health. Staying hydrated during and after physical activity can help reduce joint and back pain. Hydration can work wonders for your mind and body!

Rest & Sleep

★ The Scoop

Getting enough sleep every night is a no-brainer and will help you perform well in sports and school. In fact, you won't be able to get As in class if you don't get enough "Zs" at night! Research indicates that teenagers require 9 to 9½ hours of sleep every night in order to grow, stay healthy, and be alert the next day. Yet few teens actually get more than 7 hours of sleep! Not OK!

Each stage of sleep has its own benefits; therefore, you need enough time to move through each stage. Sleep activity ranges from light to deep sleep and dreaming. Many people get stuck in the first sleep stage when drifting off to sleep, which cuts into their actual sleep time. But you can change this if you eliminate habits that prohibit a good night's sleep and practice relaxation techniques.

So read, take a bath, or write in a journal before bed—all activities that help you wind down.

★ Ashanti's Question: Too Tired

I get tired during the day, and sometimes I fall asleep in class. It's embarrassing. But I can't help that I'm tired! Even though I fall asleep easily at night, I end up waking up thinking about stuff. What can I do to sleep through the night so I can stay awake during class?!

Isabel Says: It sounds kind of out there, but my mom taught me how to meditate and do deep-breathing exercises before bed, and it helps a lot. So every night at 9 p.m., I stop what I'm doing, go to my room, and just sit with my eyes closed for about 15 minutes while I take super deep breaths. I get so relaxed, and it's much easier to sleep soundly.

Helpful Hint

Avoid stimulants such as caffeine, chocolate, or sugar after 4 p.m. These will interfere with your ability to fall asleep at a reasonable hour, or may cause you to wake up within 30 minutes of falling asleep!

☞ Expert's Point of View

Tips and Advice from Dr. Stuart Cohen

Some teens don't sleep enough, but others actually sleep too much! Sleeping too much can cause you to feel groggy and lethargic throughout the day, and may even lead to headaches and depression. Avoid sleeping more than 9½ hours a night.

Sports & Fitness

Go team!

Staying fit is important if you want to enjoy life from the time we're teenagers until we're 80 years old. Our doctor says that people who don't exercise can have weak bones, heart problems, and become overweight. Also, couch potatoes feel tired, lethargic, and bored. That's why we both exercise.

★ Kiki's Question: Motivation

It seems like it's impossible for me to get motivated to exercise. I go to the gym for a few weeks, but then I just get lazy and stop. I get mad at myself and think I should start up again, but I'm like, "What's the point?" since I'll just quit again. Then I feel like I wasted all kinds of time. Is there any way to stay motivated?

Girl to Girl

Hate all the eyes on you at the gym? Work out at home to a DVD! They range from aerobics to kickboxing to Tai Chi, and are great for every fitness level!

Emily Says: Beating yourself up is not going to get you anywhere! Being so negative will actually discourage you from exercising. When I need to motivate, I remind myself why I want to work out. Do I want to perform better in my soccer games? Have I been feeling really tired lately? Knowing why you want to exercise is the driving force that keeps you jumping rope, even though you'd rather be taking a nap.

Isabel Says: Every girl's motivators are different. And there are days when I sleep in and skip going to the gym. When that happens, I just remind myself to get back on track the next day. A tip that works for me is to keep a workout calendar. I check off every day I exercise and write what I did.

★ Ashanti's Question: Yoga

What's the deal with yoga? It's gotten really trendy at my school, but I think it looks kind of boring. Is it just meditation or what? Can yoga really get me in good shape?

Isabel Says: You're right, Ashanti—yoga has gotten really popular with celebrities like Jennifer Aniston and Gwyneth Paltrow, and that's because it is an amazing workout with tons of benefits! Doing yoga regularly gives you long, lean muscles; increases flexibility; reduces stress; and improves your posture. No more slouching!

In a yoga session, you will hold various postures—called asanas—while focusing on breathing, balance, alignment, and different muscle groups. The result is a really toned, defined body. You should definitely try it!

Emily Says: Hey Ashanti, I used to think yoga looked lame too.

Helpful Hints

Weight training gives you more muscle mass and makes your muscles stronger. But don't worry, you won't start looking like a bodybuilder! Lifting weights a few times a week will give your arms and legs a subtle shape and definition, which looks really good—and really feminine. Plus, muscle mass actually burns fat. Even if you're just sitting there watching TV, your muscles are burning up calories. Total bonus!

Lots of sitting around, right? But then my soccer coach suggested that my team take a yoga class, because he said it would help us control our bodies, and learn focus and balance. And it was really cool! It was a great workout, and I felt a lot more calm and centered afterward.

I guess there's a reason yoga has been around for more than 3,000 years!

☞ Expert's Point of View

Tips and Advice from Fitness Expert Lisa K

Always put safety first when it comes to exercising. This includes wearing the right shoes, caring for blisters, sitting out when you are injured, and having someone spot you when lifting weights. Exercising with caution also includes warming up, cooling down, and stretching before and after your workout.

However, even if you take precautions, it is still possible to get injured during athletic activity. If you ever feel a pop in one of your joints or your lower back hurts, stop what you are doing, tell a parent or your coach, and put ice on the affected area. Taking immediate action can facilitate healing and prevent a trip to the emergency room.

Though it is frustrating, some injuries require you to take a week or more off to heal. This is a must! Exercising when injured will only cause further damage, which is counterproductive to your health goals.

Emotional Issues

Hugs make everything better!

S ome of the most difficult changes we have to deal with during puberty are the emotional ones. Emotional issues can be hard to manage, because we can't always explain them, we just feel them. The feelings that sneak up on girls during puberty can make us feel alone, confused, and out of control.

Isabel Says: Ew, I don't want to picture any of my classmates in their underwear! I say, forget you're making a school presentation. Just pretend you're talking to a bunch of friends about whatever. Stay focused, but be casual.

Something about puberty turns nice girls into jealous trolls! Of course, a little jealousy is normal and understandable. Just keep it in check, because if you let it get out of hand you will lose friends and feel pretty awful about yourself.

🖝 Expert's Point of View

Tips and Advice from Therapist Catherine Butler

One of the most difficult aspects of managing the emotions that accompany puberty is the feeling that life will always be hard. But it's not true—and as bad as you ever feel, it is important to have perspective. Having perspective means that you understand that your current state is not permanent.

For example, maybe you are upset because you are being teased for having small breasts. See the situation in a positive light. Remind yourself that you are still growing and developing, and you can make up for your size with how you dress and the bra you wear. This helps you see that nothing is hopeless.

Indeed, gaining perspective is a crucial tool to have in order to navigate the murky waters of puberty. Without perspective, life feels complicated, lonely, and scary. So, practice having perspective the next time you hear yourself say "never" or "always." Thinking this way is an exaggeration of the facts. And puberty is hard enough without exaggeration!

Mood Swings

You're up, you're down, you're a normal teenager! Mood swings are par for the course during puberty. They can be extremely frustrating for you, and for those around you. But it's not you, exactly—it's the hormones your body releases during puberty. Of course, the day-to-day stress of school, peer pressure, and changing roles within your family definitely cause mood swings to be exaggerated. However, though you may not have control over your feelings, you do have control over how you deal with them.

Girl to Girl

Sleep is important to staying rational. When you're tired and worn out, you will find your mood swings are way worse. You might freak out if a teacher corrects you or if your best friend forgets to call you back.

So make sure you are getting the recommended 9 hours of sleep a night. A good night's sleep will keep you calm and level-headed.

Learning how to channel the flood of emotions that hit you at any given moment may take some practice, but it is well worth the effort. After all, you don't want to become the hormonal monster depicted in lame teen comedies, do you? Of course not! So you will need to develop coping skills for when you are sent reeling into the emotional extremes of puberty.

★ Abbey's Question: The Blues

How do I know whether I am depressed or just feeling down in the dumps?

Isabel Says: I was down for a while and Catherine Butler gave me a handout that helped me sort out whether I was depressed or just sad. Here are some questions you should ask yourself to tell the difference: Have you been sad every day for 2 weeks or longer? Do you feel empty inside and like there is no point to anything? Have you lost or gained weight? Do you have trouble sleeping, or sleep too much? Do you feel guilty for things that aren't your fault? Is it hard to concentrate or make decisions? Do you ever think about killing yourself? If you answered "yes" to 5 or more, you may be depressed and in need of treatment.

Helpful Hint

When you are suffering from depression or anxiety, eating a healthy diet, drinking plenty of water, avoiding caffeine, and getting regular exercise will dramatically improve how you feel both emotionally and physically.

☞ Expert's Point of View

Tips and Advice from Therapist Catherine Butler

Use of antidepressants to treat teenagers is controversial, but sometimes necessary. If your depression is severe, your family and doctor should discuss all treatment options, including the possibility of medication and the help of a great counselor.

Eating Disorders

We live in a world where body image is constantly being distorted. Models and celebrities create our body-image standards, and yet even they are always being accused of being fat!

Helpful Hint

Eating disorders often develop in girls who feel like they have no control over their lives. Their parents tell them what activities to participate in or what clothes to wear. This can be incredibly frustrating, and so girls turn toward what they can control—food. If you feel like your life is out of control, talk to your parents about giving you more control over the decisions that directly affect you.

With all this pressure, we have to pay close attention to our thoughts and feelings about beauty and health so that we are able to catch ourselves (and our friends) when the desire to be thin turns into a dangerous obsession.

Eating disorders develop over time, and always have warning signs, such as becoming obsessed with weight, calories, food, dieting, appearance, and never being happy. Learn to recognize these.

Girls as young as 6 and women as old as 76 have reported suffering from eating disorders. If you have one, you are not alone, but you do need help.

★ Emani's Question: Making Myself Sick

I feel like I have been trying to lose weight but nothing works. I am still fat. I can't stand to gain one more pound, so I eat my lunch in the bathroom and then immediately throw it up. I feel like I will stop doing this once I get a handle on my weight, but I wonder if it's a problem?

Isabel Says: We know you must be worried, so the best thing to do is be honest with your doctor so you can get this figured out.

Therapist Catherine Butler says bulimia is when a person eats a lot and then throws up because they feel bad about eating so much. Teens who throw up so often will ruin their teeth, esophagus, and throat. And, if left untreated, bulimia can be fatal. So, please Emani, talk to a parent or doctor, or call the Eating Disorders Awareness and Prevention hotline at 1-800-931-2237.

Girl to Girl

Many girls with eating disorders use food to self-medicate when they are sad or anxious. So if you notice a friend in distress, reach out to her so she knows help is out there.

Emily Says: It makes me sad that wanting to be thin makes you feel like you don't deserve to eat lunch with the rest of the kids. Isabel is so right—you definitely need to address this problem. Bulimia is a serious sickness that keeps people from ever being happy with their weight and shape!

★ Aleah's Question: Obsessed

My friend is totally obsessed with her appearance. She's always finding mirrors and windows and criticizing how she looks. She talks a lot about wanting plastic surgery to fix her nose or liposuction to get rid of her fat. Sometimes she even says that she'd rather be dead than look the way she does. She's so pretty—I don't know if she really means that stuff. Should I be worried about her?

Emily Says: Aleah, our expert Catherine Butler says lots of girls stress out about parts of their bodies that they don't like, but if it's really severe, it might be an issue called body dysmorphic disorder (BDD). BDD affects 2 percent of Americans—70 percent of whom are under age 18. BDD makes people obsessed with a minor aspect of their appearance—and sometimes the flaw is totally imagined! Without treatment, people with BDD may take drastic measures to alter their appearance, so your friend should talk to a doctor, who can steer her in the right direction.

Helpful Hint

Untreated depression and anxiety can lead to an eating disorder—especially binge eating and bulimia. In both these states, a person feels as if she has a giant hole inside her that can only be filled by food. The shame she feels afterward causes her to vomit or abuse herself—even cut herself to release some of the pain. Getting treatment for depression and anxiety can dramatically decrease the need to act out in these harmful ways.

Isabel Says: Aleah, every girl has parts of her body she doesn't love, but there is a real difference between that and BDD, which can cause depression and social anxiety. Urge your friend to visit a trained professional!

☞ Expert's Point of View

Tips and Advice from Therapist Catherine Butler

Recovery is essential to the health of the person affected by an eating disorder. In fact, people who do not get treatment can die from their condition. Eating disorders are a painful existence for the sufferer and agonizing for friends and family to watch. However, once treatment has begun, there is light at the end of the tunnel.

Treatment for an eating disorder may include hospitalization, different forms of therapy, and medication. The goal is to rid the person of her fear or addiction to food, and to help her value her life and to eat—and keep down—a varied diet. This can take many years, and there are often setbacks and relapses.

Most important to know is that people who suffer from eating disorders have a sickness. They are not just craving attention or seeking to drop a couple of pounds. They have a serious illness that requires treatment.